Table of Contents

Before You Get Started

Why are you interested in starting a small business? What are your motivations? Before you let your thoughts even get out of the starting gate and start racing, you need to write down and evaluate the reasons behind your desire to run your own business. In addition, you should look at your own personal characteristics, conditions, skills and experience and determine if they are compatible with assuming the role of small business owner. Next, look for a niche for your business and analyze your market.

Take a Personal Inventory

Take a minute and write down the reasons you want to own your own business. These may, but certainly do not have to, include the following:

- Freedom from a 9 to 5 work schedule
- Not being told what you have to do any more
- Improving your economic position
- Boredom
- Desire to provide the marketplace with a unique product or service that you feel there is a need for

Next, take a look at your personal characteristics and honestly evaluate whether you have the personality traits and physical conditioning necessary to operate the specific business you are considering. For instance, are you a leader? Are you in good health? Running your own business can require working 12 to 16 hours per day six days a week in the beginning. Are you emotionally grounded? Becoming your own boss will be rewarding, but it will also be stressful. Can you afford to lower your standard of living until your business becomes established? Does your family understand the consequences of the undertaking? If

4

you are considering starting your own business, it is a good idea to start it in a field in which you have some experience. Have you ever worked in a business that is similar to the one you are considering? You will need to know enough about the business to be able to determine if prospective employees meet the requirements for the job openings that you are filling. As a business owner, you will also need to be familiar with good business practices. Do you know what basic business skills you will need and so you possess them? Have you had any business classes in school? Have you ever been in a managerial role?

Look for a Niche

Dictionary.com defines the word niche as "a place or position suitable for a person or thing" or "a distinct segment of a market". In other words, you are looking for a business that feels good to you and that you will be happy starting and developing and you are also looking for a specific need in the population that you can meet. To determine if your particular idea is workable, write down the answers to the following questions:

- Name the product or service that you will be selling.
- Describe the unfulfilled need in the marketplace that you are addressing.
- Describe the existing market for your product or service – particularly, analyzing whether or not demand exceeds supply.
- Determine whether or not your product or service can be competitive in the current marketplace based on its unique characteristics.

Market Analysis

After you believe you have identified a niche for yourself in the business world, that is, you believe your product and service can be competitive, you need to take a closer look at the market you will be serving.

Who will your customers be and what do they need from you? Do you know the exact geographic area you will be serving? Are there any particular customs or religious beliefs that you should be aware of? Can you offer products and services at prices that your customers are willing to pay and will your products and services are competitive in price and quality to what is already available in the marketplace? Have you developed a promotional program that targets your particular market effectively?

Top Ten Business Mistakes

1. Not Enough Capital

Assessing small business start up costs is tricky. Most business owners project operating costs to the point of breakeven. (The breakeven point is when the daily or monthly income from the business equals the daily or monthly expenses to stay in business.) What start up costs should include is all the costs required to open for business, and all the operating costs to the point of profitability. This means instead of figuring start up costs to the 'breakeven point,' the point should be when the owner estimates he or she will be able to get paid the minimum salary required.

Estimating start up costs should include these categories:

- Start Up Purchase Costs: Equipment, furniture, insurance, business licenses, etc.

- Reoccurring Services Costs – utilities, telephones, outsourcing, insurance, business licenses, etc. (Notice that some start up costs are also reoccurring costs.)

- Advertising/Marketing Costs – Here are some of the biggest pitfalls for small business owners. Even big businesses often have no idea how much they will need to spend in advertising dollars to bring in enough business. Most can only estimate this based on experience. .

- Product or Inventory Costs
  The purchase and/or financing costs of inventory.

- Holding Costs (of Products or Inventory)

if inventory is required, housing, insuring, and handling inventory can become expensive.

2. Spending Too Much

While this seems to be easy to avoid, this is one of the most common start up mistakes. One distinct advantage of the home based business is low overhead, but many of these business owners buy services they don't really need, or max out their credit cards on equipment, computers, cell phones, PDAs, copiers, printers, and other gadgets

3. Lack of Knowledge

Most people do not lack the knowledge about the industry they start a business in, but about business in general. Just because you know your stuff at your job, does not necessarily mean you could succeed on your own.

There is an enormous amount of information required to operate a business.

- Administrative Techniques – including employee, outsourcing, task assignment, prioritizing, and organization.
- Advertising – types, effectiveness, costs, tracking methods, creation,
- Bookkeeping – record keeping
- Financial Analogy and Forecasting – profit and loss statement and balance sheet interpretation
- Law
- Marketing
- Personnel Management
- Product or Service

4. Not Adequately Defining the Market

A small business can easily exhaust all capital in advertising. Whether it's traditional print ads or pay per click, if the target market is not reached, the mistake could be realized too late.

5. Mismanagement
New small business owners often start without a plan or fail to follow their plan. Learning to prioritize, organize, and improvise can be new to people who have not worked in previous management positions.

6. Not Having Contacts and Services in Place

There is nothing worse than needing a contact for a business transaction, and losing the deal before you can find the help. Having no or poor subcontract services can leave you scrambling to find help. This search alone can be enough to hurt a small business.

7. Ineffective Marketing

This is mistake can include inefficient marketing, poor content, ill timed advertising, wrong target market, and overspending, and many more.

Learning your market and how to get business could be the most important aspect. Having more than enough business can compensate for mistakes or shortcomings in other areas.

8. Failing to Rectify Mistakes

Sometimes business owners fail to recognize mistakes, but even worse, when they do spot them, they do nothing. This happens for several reasons.

If the business owner has come from an employment position, many times he or she does not fully grasp that the buck now stops with them. They are used to someone else taking the responsibility. These owners often become immobilized in the face of a blunder, and do nothing. This is where a business mentor can be a lifesaver. Every new business owner should have one or more seasoned business owners to turn to in turbulent waters. Preferably, this person should be a home-based business owner who is or has been in the same or a similar industry. Before you go into business, mentor contacts should be established.

9. Refusing to Delegate

Small business owners are usually 'take charge' people. They know their businesses better than anyone else and can do most every job. In the beginning and as their business grows, these owners often retain duties and responsibilities far beneath their capabilities and not in the best health of the business. As a small business owner, you must decide which jobs would be better off delegated or outsourced.

10. Time Management

Time is money. There are so many distractions in today's world of business and a home based business is no exception. Few people manage their time effectively. All the conveniences such as cell phones, PDA's, email, RSS News feeds, the Internet, online meetings, software updates, and online bill pay, can consume your time if not used wisely. The home based business can even face additional interruptions from family and chores.

Starting a business takes enormous energy. You can't afford to just coast along, go through the motions, or get burnt out. If you feel like quitting, you can' give a two week notice and leave, without losing your investment and future income. Many new small business owners cannot even afford vacations or holidays for several years.

You have to be aware.
Again, the employee might not be trained to look for new opportunities. As a business owner, this is imperative. The chance to get new customers, move into a new market, offer a new product or service, could be missed if you're not aware.

You need to adjust to uncertainty.
As an employee you are pretty much guaranteed a regular paycheck. As an entrepreneur, there's no guarantee.

You will deal with the uncertainty of the fluctuations of the economy, slow accounts receivable, surprise expenses, loss of clients, changes in technology, and trends.

Start-Up Business

When you have successfully navigated through the sea of possibilities and have chosen a particular type of business and a product or service that you believe will be competitive, you must begin to consider the financial and legal aspects of running a small business. Let's start with the basics. What are you going to call your company and what kind of organizational structure will it have?

Naming Your Business

Many times it is harder to name a new business than we think the process will be. It seems like you should be able to come up with something catchy that you like the ring of and run with it, but it isn't that simple. Before you name your business you have to determine its organizational structure. Many states require sole proprietors to use their real name as their business name, unless they legally file for a trade name or some other type of fictitious name. Next you have to determine if the name you use for your actual business, its trade name, will be the same as its full legal name. Finally, you must investigate the possibility that someone else has already chosen that name, and, if so, what their rights are to use that name in the area you will be serving. Trade names are registered through the Secretary of State's Office in each state and for wider coverage through the United States Patent and Trademark Office. The first step in determining whether or not your proposed name is already in use is to use the USPTO's online system which allows you to search all that state and federal trademark registers.

If your business will be operating on the Web, your trade name might be your domain name. Domain names are not registered with local or state government, but are sold through a number of online businesses. Usually these businesses will allow you to search for your chosen domain name to see if it is already in use before you purchase it.

Domains under **.com**, **.org**, and **.net** can be registered via a number of different registrars. Check out the prices and plans offered by the various registrars. The registrars have recently been lowering their prices and making the process of registering and updating domains more convenient.

Be sure you go to a legitimate, accredited registrar. There have been some scams and rip offs in domain registration. Make sure you or someone in your organization is listed as the owner and administrative contact. A list of registrars with consumer reviews can be found at www.findaregister.com.

The cost of registering domain names ranges from eight to forty dollars per year. Price is *not* the only option to consider. Make sure they have a history of good customer support and you understand the terms of service.

Types of Business Organization

Deciding on what type of organizationally structure to use for your new business has far-reaching implications and should be done in conjunction with an accountant and an attorney. The following factors should be considered when making this decision:

- How big your business will be
- The type of business you will be operating
- How much control you wish to have over day-to-day operations
- Your capability to deal with a more complex structure
- Vulnerability to lawsuits
- Tax implications
- Expected profits and losses
- Desire to reinvest earnings

- Accessibility of cash

Sole Proprietorships

Most small businesses at least start out as sole proprietorships. These businesses are owned by one person who usually is responsible for the day-to-day operation of the business. He or she owns all of the assets and profits of the business, but is also completely liable for any debts or legal actions.

Advantages	Disadvantages
Easy and cheap	Unlimited liability
No sharing of authority	Business and personal assets in danger
Can keep or reinvest income	Capital may be hard to come by and may be limited to personal loans or savings
Profits are directly applied to personal taxes	Hard to attract high quality employees due to lack of advancement opportunities
Easy to disband	Some employee benefits are not directly deductible from business income tax return

Partnerships

A partnership allows two or more people to share the ownership of a business. There are three basic types of partnerships: a general partnership, a limited partnership, and a joint venture. A general partnership allows partners to divide evenly authority and liability as well as profits and losses. Equal shares are assumed unless otherwise stated in a partnership agreement. Limited partnerships limit the liability of each partner to the extent of their investment in the business, as well as limiting their authority to the same extent. This organizational structure tends to encourage investors for short-term projects and is not used very often in the retail and service industries. A joint venture is a general partnership that is just intended to last for a limited time period or a specific project. If the partners wish to work together again, they must be recognized as a specific type of partnership after dissolving and distributing the assets of the current joint venture.

Advantages	Disadvantages
Easy to establish	Jointly and individually liable for all partners
Easier to raise capital	All profits are shared
Profits are credited towards partners personal tax returns	Decisions must be made jointly and disagreements are always possible
Prospective employees may be intrigued by the idea of becoming a partner	Some employee benefits are not deductible from the business income tax return
Partners can complement each other with their personalities and management techniques	Partnerships have a limited life span and may end upon the withdrawal or death of a partner

Corporations

A corporation must be chartered in the state in which its primary headquarters are located. It is considered to be a legal entity in itself and is not connected to those who own it for liability purposes. It can be taxed, sued, and enter into contracts. It is owned by its shareholders who elect a board of directors to oversee the major policy decisions. These decisions must be documented. It does not have a limited life span and can continue to operate if and when ownership changes for any reason. Small corporations may be operated on a less formal basis, but records must still be kept.

Advantages	Disadvantages
Shareholders enjoy limited liability	More complex and costly
Capital can be raised through stock sales	Officers can be held personally liable
Benefits for officers and employees can be deducted from business income tax returns	Monitored closely be local, state, and federal entities
	May result in higher taxes (Dividends paid to shareholders are not deductible and thus end up being taxed twice)

Subchapter S Corporations

This classification is available for tax purposes only and allows shareholders to treat their earnings and profits just like dividends and funnel them through their personal tax returns. The shareholder must meet the standards of "reasonable compensation" if they work for the corporation.

Limited Liability Corporation (LLC)

This is a new type of business structure that allows a company to take advantage of the limited liability features of a corporation and the tax benefits and flexibility of a partnership. The owners are termed as "members" of the corporation and the duration of the association of the members is determined upon organization, although it can be continued upon a favorable vote by its members. A LLC must not have more than two of the four major characteristics of a corporation which follow:

- Limited liability for members to the extent of their investment
- Unlimited lifespan
- Centralized operations
- Free transferability of interests.

Records

Are you fully aware of all the laws that govern the industry that you plan to become a part of? Will you be affected by OSHA requirements? Do you use any hazardous materials that may be subject to regulations? Are you familiar with you state's workmen's compensation laws? What about federal regulations regarding withholding taxes and social security? You will need to hire the appropriate personnel and consult a lawyer in order to keep abreast of all the business laws you will be expected to obey.

A small business requires vigilant organization for records management. Having an effective system in place at the beginning can save you big headaches in the future. There are customer records, invoices, bills, purchase orders, bank statements, credit card statements, receipts, and passwords. Aim for a paperless office. While we have not yet quite reached a hundred per cent digital business, you'll find that by banking online, receiving e-bills, and scanning documents to disk, using point of sale systems, and managing

17

databases, you can become more efficient and conserve space.

Bank Account

While a bank account is your means of moving your money, this is also the recording of most financial transactions. Because of this, opening a business bank account is one of the first things you should do when starting a business.

A business bank account can be linked to bookkeeping software, Internet banking, merchant accounts, and business debit cards.

Maintaining a business bank account gives your new business needed credibility. There are several considerations for choosing the bank and type of account for your small business; such as transaction costs, maintenance fees, services available, lines of credit, debit card options, Internet banking services and fees available, location, merchant services, borrowing options, and the availability of a personal commercial banker (bank personnel trained in small business services.).

If you are a Limited Company, Partnership, Corporation, you must have a separate business bank account.

Online banking services are essential to today's small business. You can check records of transactions, move funds, and pay bills twenty four hours a day, all from your computer.

Licenses and Permits

Business licensing differs from country to country but the following list displays the common issues that must be addressed by the small business owner.

18

1) Business Licenses
   This is the main document that you must acquire in order to perform basic business functions and file taxes.

2) Occupational or Professional Licenses
   Most states require specific occupations and professions to obtain licensure before they can begin working. They may also be required to renew this licensure on a regular basis and/or enroll in continuing education classes to update their skills. The occupations and professions that are regulated vary from building contractors to physicians to appraisers to accountants to barbers to real estate agents to auctioneers to private investigators to bill collectors to cosmetologists, just to name a few. Always check with your state of residence to determine if your particular profession or occupation is regulated.

3) Product Licenses
   Most states require special licenses to sell liquor, lottery tickets, gasoline, or guns.

4) Income Tax
   If the state or locality your business is in has an income tax, then you will be responsible for obtaining an employer identification number from your Department of Revenue or Treasury.

5) Sales Tax
   If you are going to be selling retail goods, you will also have to obtain a state sales tax license.

6) Company Name Registration

You will need to register the name your company will be doing business under with at least the state you are operating in. If you plan to do business outside of the state, you will need to consider registering the name elsewhere, including with the federal trademark office.

7) Unemployment Payments

If you employ others, you will be expected to make unemployment insurance payment to your state.

8) EIN Number

Most business types, excluding sole proprietorships, are required to file for a federal tax identification number or EIN, regardless of whether they have employees or not.

9) Other Federal Regulations

Most businesses do not require any other federal licenses or permits. However some industries are regulated by federal agencies that determine the requirements that companies operating in that industry must meet to do business. Some of these industries are investment advising, drug manufacturing, meat processing, broadcasting, ground transportation, and the selling, of alcohol, tobacco, or firearms.

Risk Protection

As you start your adventure into small business ownership, you will need to protect yourself and your business against such things as fire, theft, robbery, vandalism, and accident liability. Contact a local insurance agent for recommendations as to what types of coverage your particular business will require. Another option is to visit the internet site www.Insure.com which offers a Small Business Liability Tool. This interactive feature allows you to choose the type of business you are interested in starting and informs you as to the types of risk that particular profession faces.

Record Keeping

You must be aware of what financial reports you are required to prepare, how to prepare them, and who will prepare them. Payroll records, including tax reports and payments, must also be completed in an efficient manner. Complete records of sales and expenses along with accounts payable and receivable are indispensable and must be kept accurately from the start-up phase until the dissolution of the company.

Merchandise

If your new business will be selling or making a product or products, do you know exactly what these items will be? If you new business is providing a service, do you know exactly what that service will encompass? A merchandise plan must be developed based upon estimated sales that will determine the amount of inventory or supplies you will need upon opening your doors for business. When you have determined what you need and how much of it, look for reliable suppliers who are more than happy to help you through the start-up phase of your new business venture. Compare the prices, quality, and credit terms of all suppliers that you are considering.

Location

When starting a small business, you must consider what the optimum location for your particular endeavor would be and come as close as possible to finding the perfect place. Location is a major factor in the success or failure of any business and yours will be no exception. A good location can help a business that may be struggling financially to survive, whereas, a poor location can result in even a well-managed business failing.

You must consider a location that is convenient for the customer base you plan to serve. Once you have narrowed down your search area you must look for buildings that met your needs as they are or can be modified at a reasonable cost. You will want to consider renting or leasing and even leasing with an option to buy. There is usually far more freedom in negotiation a commercial lease than in renting a residential space and leasing without committing yourself to ownership may be the best choice for fledgling businesses as they do not know whether the location will be optimum as of yet.

Every lease agreement should be written and should contain at least the following information:

- Amount of rent that will be paid by the tenant (possible increases and the basis for these increases should also be spelled out)

- Length of the lease (conditions necessary for renewal should also be included)
  Whether or not utilities are included in the rent payment and if not exactly what utilities the tenant is responsible for
- Maintenance expenses, property taxes, and insurance costs that the tenant may or may not be required to pay

- Any deposits required

- Detailed description of the area being leased including the square footage, parking facilities, and any other perks that might come with it

- List of improvements that the landlord has promised to complete

- Any statements made by the landlord or his agent regarding foot traffic, average utility costs, restrictions on renting to competitors, etc.

- Zoning regulations

- Restrictions or subleasing or assigning the lease if necessary

- Terms for termination of the agreement by either party.

Zoning

When you are considering where to locate your new business do not overlook the zoning regulations that may affect the properties that you are considering. You can call your local planning department to ask exactly how each property is zoned. This is important because zoning laws may place restrictions on the height and overall size of buildings, the percentage of the lot they may be built upon, the kinds of facilities that must be included based on the property's intended use, and the distance between the front, back, and side property lines that any structure must maintain.

Zoning regulations are not easily changed and, therefore, it is best to know upfront what the regulations are concerning its intended use. Properties are usually zoned as residential, commercial, industrial, agricultural, or recreational. Changing these classifications require a period of public notice and having the variance approved by various government agencies.

Financing

A great number of small businesses fail each year because of insufficient funds. Too many people try to start their business without enough money to support them through the first few lean months. Consider how much money you have access to now, how much money you will need to start your business, and how much money you will need to stay in business.

Assets and Liabilities

Take a good look at your current assets and liabilities.

Assets	Liabilities
Cash on hand/Other liquid assets	Accounts payable
Savings Accounts	Notes payable
Stocks, bonds, securities	Contracts payable
Accounts/notes receivable	Taxes
Real Estate	Real estate loans
Life insurance (cash value of policies)	Other liabilities
Automobile/other vehicles	

Start-Up Cost Estimates

After you have a good idea of what your current financial status is, take a look at how much money starting your new business will require. You will need to write down an educated guesstimate in for each of the following categories:

- Decorating, remodeling
- Fixtures, equipment
- Installation of fixtures, equipment
- Services, supplies
- Basic Inventory
- Legal, professional fees
- Licenses, permits
- Telephone, utility deposits
- Insurance
- Signs
- Advertising
- Unanticipated Expenses

Monthly Expenses

After you have determined how much money will be required just to open the doors of your small business, you need to calculate your expenses per month to keep the business going. Upon opening for business you will need enough money on hand to cover these expenses for the first three months.

- Your living expenses
- Employee wages
- Rent
- Advertising
- Supplies

- Utilities
- Insurance
- Taxes
- Maintenance
- Delivery/transportation
- Miscellaneous

Getting the Money You Need

Now that you are aware of the financial investment that will be necessary to start and operate your own business, where will you find the money? First, of course, look at your own personal savings and credit cards. If this is not sufficient, you may have the option of asking family and/or friends for help. They can often provide you with interest free or low interest loans. Your next option is to go to the bank or credit union and try to obtain a small business loan. Finally, there are venture capital firms whose sole purpose is to help companies grow in exchange for a share in their ownership.

Obtaining a Loan

It is not necessarily true that small business people have difficult time borrowing money from financial institutions. Banks and credit unions are in the business of lending money and that is what they want to do. However, they want to loan their money to people who are likely to pay it back; those that they deem a "good risk".

To be successful in getting a loan approved you must be organized and have a thorough loan proposal prepared that addresses all the pertinent questions that your lender might have. Presenting yourself and your ideas well is often the key to success.

In addition, if your lending institution turns your proposal down, you have the option of asking that it be submitted to the Small Business

Administration (SBA). SBA can guarantee up to 80% of a small business loan if the proposal meets their standards: repayment ability form business's cash flow, good character, leadership capacity, collateral, and owner's equity contribution. All principals who own 20% or more of the business are required to personally guarantee all SBA loans and the lender must agree to loan the money with the SBA's guarantee.

Writing a Loan Proposal

A good loan proposal should include the following information:

1) General Information
   A. Business Name
   B. Name and Social Security Number of Principals
   C. Business Address
   D. Purpose of Loan
   E. Exact Amount of Money Being Requested

2) Business Description
   A. History of the Business (if applicable)
   B. Nature of the Business
   C. Number of Employees
   D. Current Assets
   E. Organizational Structure

3) Management Profile
   A. Short Biography of Each Principal
4) Market Information
   A. Define Products and Markets
   B. Identify Competition
   C. Explain How You Plan to Compete in the Marketplace

       D. Profile Customers

  5) Financial Information
       A. Financial Statements, Balance Sheets, and Income
           Sheets for the Past 3 Years
       B. Projected Balance and Income Sheets for the Current
           Year
       C. Personal Financial Statements for Yourself and All
           Principals
       D. Any Collateral You Are Willing to Put Up

Types of Business Loans

There are two basic types of business loans: short term and long term. Short term loans have a maturity of up to one year and are most often working capital loans, accounts receivable loans, or lines of credit. Long term loans have maturities that are more than one year but usually less than seven years. Loans for real estate and equipment can have maturities of up to twenty-five years. Long term loans are used for mainly for purchasing real estate, construction, equipment, furniture and fixtures, vehicles, and other high end items.

Understand and Projecting Cash Flow

Cash flow is the movement of money in and out of your business. This cycle of cash in and out determines your business' solvency.

Cash flow analysis is the study of the cycle of your business' cash inflows and outflows, for the purpose of maintaining, managing, and forecasting cash flow.

Cash flow analysis involves examining the components of your business that affect cash flow. These are accounts receivable, inventory, accounts payable, interest, and credit terms. Performing a cash flow analysis on these separate components will help you spot cash flow issues and find ways to make improvements.

28

One way to perform a cash flow analysis is to compare the unpaid bills to the total sales due at the end of each month. If the bills are greater than the total sales due, you'll need more cash than you receive in the next month, and this will be a cash flow shortage.

Cash Flow Projection
Cash Flow Projection is to forecast how money will flow in and out of your business during a certain future time period. You need to know when your expenditures are too high, income is too low, or when you have a cash flow surplus. As part of your business plan, a Cash Flow Projection will give you a much better idea of how much capital investment your business idea needs.

Cash Flow Projection determines your credit risk.

The difference between a Cash Flow Projection and a Cash Flow Statement is that a Cash Flow Statement records cash flow for a period in the past. Both of these Cash Flow reports are important business decision-making tools for businesses, but you are only concerned with the Cash Flow Projection for your business plan. Your Cash Flow Projections should be shown monthly for a three year period as part of the Financial Plan portion of your business plan.

The Three Parts to the Cash Flow Projection
The first part details your Cash Revenues or cash income. Enter your total estimated income you expect to collect each month.

The second part is your Cash Disbursements. These are the expenses from your ledger that you expect to pay that month for each month.

The third part of the Cash Flow Projection is the Reconciliation of Cash Revenues to Cash Disbursements. This section starts with the opening balance (which is the carryover from the previous month). The current month's Revenues are added to this balance; the current month's Disbursements are subtracted, and the adjusted cash flow balance is carried over to the next month. Remember, the Closing Cash Balance is carried over to the next month.

29

Sales Forecasting
Sales forecasting is estimating what your sales will be. There are sophisticated formulas and less complex methods for sales forecasting.

If you sell several types of products and services, prepare a separate sales forecast for each one or group.

Be sure to account for factors that can affect your sales, including:

- Seasons
- Holidays
- Special Events
- Competition
- Product Availability
- Personal Issues
- Trends
- Economic Climate
- Population Changes

Create a Customer Profile
Learn about your customers. Identify who they are, why they buy, when they buy, how they buy, and where they are. You should know your target group by age, sex, location, interests, and buying habits.

Create a Competitor Profile
Find out who your competitors are and study their practices. Visit their websites or locations. Analyze everything you can; location, sales volumes, traffic patterns, hours of operation, busy periods, prices, quality of their goods and services, promotions, brochures, etc.

Estimate Your Sales for the First Year
Base your numbers as realistically as possible by estimating what your competitor are doing and what you will be doing. Be sure to note how long each one has been in business. Momentum builds in most businesses and a company on equal footing financially would need almost as much time in business to reach the same level of sales.

Consider how well your competition is doing. Determine what you will do different or better. Will you offer a better location, more convenience, lower price, be more accessible, offer better quality or better service?

Consider population and economic growth in your trading area.

Now estimate what your market share will be. Use a percentage of the total market in volume annually. Now turn this in to the appropriate dollar amount. Divide this total volume by the average sale you would expect to make per customer in one year. The result will be the number of customers you need to obtain that market share. Does this number look feasible?

Total Market Value (in money) multiplied by the *Percentage of Expected Market Share* equals *Total Revenue Forecast*

Total Revenue Forecast divided by *Average Sale per Customer* equals *Total Customers*

Developing Your Business Plan

Now that you have assembled all of this information what do you do with it? You put it into a cohesive business plan that will help you reach your goals. The process of developing this plan will bring to light any issues that you may not have considered yet. The business plan will also be a useful tool. It will become invaluable when and if you need to raise more capital for your business and give you the ability to gauge your success by allowing you to see the milestones you have reached.

Here is a general outline for a business plan:

1) Introduction
   A. Detailed description of the business and your vision for its future
   B. Organizational structure of the business and ownership
   C. Skills and experience you (and your partners, if applicable) can contribute to the business
   D. Edge your business has over its competitors

2) Marketing
   A. Products and/or services offered
   B. Customer demand
   C. Market size and locations
   D. Advertising
   E. Pricing

3) Financial Management
   A. Source and amount of initial investment
   B. Monthly operating budget
   C. Monthly expected cash flow
   D. Projected income statements and balance sheets
   E. Breakeven point
   F. Compensation

G. Accounting practices

H. Alternative approaches to any anticipated roadblocks

4) Operations

A. Day-to-day management

B. Hiring and personnel procedures

C. Insurance, lease or rent agreements

D. Necessary equipment for production

E. Delivery of products and/or services

5) Concluding Statement

A. Business goals and objectives

B. Commitment to success

Your business plan should be flexible and should be able to change as your business grows. You may wish to review your business plan with a friend or business associate to for content and structure before you present it in professional situations.

The Marketing Plan

The marketing plan section of your overall business plan will benefit you create a business plan or not. Marketing and advertising, in many forms, drives most businesses. The secret to advertising is getting the right message to the right people at the right time.

You need some basic advertising knowledge to create an accurate marketing plan.

The Brand Plan

Your brand is basically the message you want people to get when they encounter you business.

Business Cards

Despite all the Internet commerce a business card is still a valuable promotion tool. Whether you personally hand, mail, or distribute your card to someone, this simple gesture is a tangible representation of your business.

Develop a simple and impressionable logo. Have a logo contest and announce this to graphic artists via the net. You should get many to choose from. Award the winner what the standard rate of cost. Publish this same logo everywhere. On your Internet site, your email, your business card, your advertising, your product or packaging, letterhead, your vehicles, your signs, and wherever people can see it.

Your Customer
Defining your customer is paramount to succeeding in small business. A great place to start is with the who, what, why, how, when, and where of your customer. This is your customer profile.

Your Customer

Who?

- Who is your customer?
  For Example: Is your customer a business owner?
  ...homeowner? ...male? ... female? ...what age?

- Who does your prospect buy from now?

- Who will you be in your customer's eyes?

What

- What is your product or service?

- What demand are you meeting?

- What is your competitors' product?

Why?

- Why does your customer buy?

- Why will your prospect buy from you?

How?

- How does your customer find out about your specific industry?

  For example, if you are in the 24 Hour emergency drain cleaning business, most customers still turn to the phone book for help. People have drain issues at all hours, and in places where they do not have a computer. If you're thinking about avoiding the phone book and going strictly to the Internet, you might have an uphill battle.

  Remember do not try to reeducate the public. This includes attempting to change present buying behavior. Your drain cleaning company could certainly use a website in addition to the phone book advertising.

Sending out a direct mail piece advertising emergency drain cleaning might also prove ineffective. The need for your service is unplanned. Sending out a direct mail refrigerator magnet advertising your service might be more productive. People will see your name and number regularly on their refrigerator and know how to reach you when the time comes.

- How does your customer buy your product?
  Are people used to buying your product or service locally? …in stores? …on the Internet? …from direct contact?

- How are people used to paying for your product or service? …by credit card? …with cash?

- How much are people presently paying for your product or service?

- How much will you need to sell your product or service for to be competitive?

Where?

Where is your customer?
Is your customer local, regional, or worldwide?
Where is your customer when they are in the most likely place to need, want, or be reminded of your product or service? Are they in their car, on a train, or at the computer? Are they at home, at work, or somewhere else?

Your advertising will need to target your customer where they are and at the appropriate time.

When?
When does your customer buy? When is your customer most likely to buy? When is the best time to reach your customer? When they are working? When they have received their tax refund? When they are shopping, eating, or working? Is your product seasonal?

Companies spend billions of dollars researching the who, what, why, how, when, and where of consumers.

You can research statistics online, purchase information from data mining companies, or perform your own research.

Accumulating and analyzing information about your typical customer should help you develop an effective financial strategy for marketing and an advertising budget.

Decide what types of advertising are going to be the most economical for reaching your customer.

Advertising you might want to consider includes:

Internet

- Website
- Affiliate Advertising
- Pay per Click
- Press Releases

Traditional Print Advertising

- Brochures
- Direct Mail
- Newspapers
- Magazines

Internet Advertising

The Press Release

Traditional press releases are information considered to have value for the general public by the sender. These press releases are targeted towards members of the news media to deliver a message.

For many years press releases were submitted via telegraph, hand delivery, or US Mail to selected television and radio stations, newspaper and magazine newsrooms, and other media outlets. The press releases would contain news and event or product announcements.

The distribution of press releases was limited to journalists and news organizations on the sender's mailing list. These news outlets only had the ability to dispense the message to their local audience.

Every day, tens of thousands of press releases competed for a spot in print. Because news outlets have traditionally assumed the role as 'gatekeepers' of information, the assignment editors and news directors had o wade through the mountain of press releases and decide which ones were newsworthy enough to print.

Online PR

The Internet press release is delivered in real time. You can have much more control of your press releases by sending them directly to consumers and media distributors.

The news release distribution wires Business Wire, Market Wire, PrimeNewswire, PRWeb, and U.S. Newswire have developed sophisticated marketing services for press releases.

You can increase distribution with tools such as RSS feed, tracking, Keyword Optimization, social media tagging, and enhance your press release with audio, video, and interactivity.

Online Press Releases can get you more attention than what most advertising generates.

The advantages over traditional advertising are numerous. Print advertising, for example, takes more time, effort, and money. Newspaper and magazine advertising can be targeted locally, but is usually more costly, is not live, and tracking results is difficult.

However, there are businesses and situations where print advertising still has value for business.

Newspapers and Magazines

Certain businesses still do well advertising in traditional newspapers and magazines.

Your newspaper advertising strategy will depend on your type of business. The first question is: "When and in what section of the newspaper do your customers look for your type of business?"

Guidelines:

1. Over time, a smaller advertisement run repeatedly will do better than a large ad run less frequently.
Your service or product might be one that people buy when they are ready so you need to keep your name in front of them. You also build trust with repetitive exposure.

2. People shop different days of the week. Friday, Saturday and Sunday papers are more for weekend shopping. A retail business will want to focus on these days.

3. The general public looks for certain information on specific days. If your competitors are all running their ads on Wednesday, there is a reason.

Make sure you maintain your logo (brand) in all of your print advertising. This will keep you consistent even though your offer might change,

Direct Mail

Direct mail is a tried and true advertising medium. There are several advantages to direct mail:

1. Direct mail is measurable. When customers walk through the door with your mailer in hand, you can easily measure response. Some direct mail outfits will track this data for you.

2. Direct mail is inexpensive. When you are conducting a direct mail from a targeted list, this is a cost-effective use of your advertising dollar. You are getting your message to those who are genuinely interested. Each direct mail campaign should get better than the last. Using response analysis data, you should be able to analyze each promotion become more effective.

3. Direct mail is targetable. Rather than sending a generic message out to the general population, direct mail targets your audience. A direct mail company can help you gather information about your target audience.

4. Direct mail is timed and planned. *Direct mail is also the only advertising that can be guaranteed to reach its audience.*

5. Direct mail is private communication. Secret - between you and your prospect.

There are several advantages of direct mail but unless you are very experienced with this type of marketing, this is not a do-it-yourself project. Success is typically forty per cent dependent on the list, forty per cent on the offer, and twenty per cent on everything else (creative, layout, paper stock, etc.). Gain the assistance of a reputable direct mail firm, and enjoy the rewards.

- Make sure everyone has seen the artwork before you go to print. This includes the direct mail service. They will check all postal regulations to save money and avoid costly mistakes in size, bar coding etc.

- If possible, use letter-size mail to save money on postage.

- Automate your mailing lists to take advantage of postal barcodes. This improves speed of delivery and allows you to take advantage of postal discounts.

- Make your sales message personalized and targeted to each individual as much as possible. This will greatly improve the response rate.

- Keep your mailing list updated to delete duplicates and bad addresses. This will reduce your postage costs and the number of returned mailing pieces.

- Print "Address Correction" endorsements on your envelopes to help maintain your mailing lists.

- Send a post card to your entire mailing list once a year via First Class postage. The U.S. Postal Service will inform you of undeliverable addresses free of charge. This is an economical way to help update your mailing lists.

Radio and Television

Radio and television stations have relied on ratings by groups such as Neilson and Arbitron to make their pitch. Though convincing, there are no guarantees of who, or if even anyone, will hear or see your advertising or information.

Print advertising and the older electronic media still have their place, but Internet advertising is quickly becoming a strategic form of more effective results oriented marketing.

Yellow Page Advertising

According to the Yellow Pages Association, 99% of adults in the United States are familiar with the Yellow Pages; 49% refer to it in a typical week; and 87% are likely to make a purchase after consulting the Yellow Pages. No other form of advertising can claim such a high follow-through.

The Yellow Pages Association also tells us that people who are most likely to use the Yellow Pages are affluent, well-educated, technologically savvy, and willing to try new brands if they have the right information in front of them. They are also value shoppers who are willing to spend more to get more value. Isn't this the kind of consumer that most businesses wish to attract through their marketing efforts?

The Yellow Pages extend the reach of other advertising media making them an essential part of many advertising campaigns. According to a 2006 Media Impact Study conducted by TNS, 12.5% of consumers utilized direct mail. 2.5% used direct mail and the Yellow Pages and 17.6% used the Yellow Pages alone. Thus, by combining different types of advertising, a business can reach a much larger portion of the population. This is true for other types of advertising as well, as shown below:

There are even different types of Yellow Pages directories being published today. An area-wide or overlay directory combines areas that are currently served by multiple directories into one larger directory area. A suburban or neighborhood directory serves a specific geographic area that is already covered by a larger directory. A special interest or niche directory is targeted at specific consumer markets. Business-to-business directories cater to the purchasing needs of business customers. Knowledge of the existence of these different types of directories allows businesses to target their advertising more effectively.

Yellow page ads are sold on an annual basis and their price is based on the advertising space you choose and the circulation size of the particular directory. A basic one –line listing comes free with your business telephone service. However, you can upgrade your listing ranging from just using bold-face type in your one-line ad to purchasing a full-page advertisement with color. Ads are arranged under each heading in the directory from biggest to smallest based on seniority. Therefore, the first full-page advertisement that you see in each section is the advertiser who has had their full-page ad the longest. This is the same for the ¾-page ads, and the ½-page ads as well. If at any time you choose to upgrade or downgrade the size of your ad, your advertisement will be added to the end of the section.

There are certain things that you must include in a Yellow Pages advertisement in order to make it effective. First, your headline should identify your company and the area you serve. Second, you need to state as clearly and precisely as possible what your business does. Make sure that you include any products or services that make you unique among your competitors. Third, advertise your incentives to customers, such as free estimates, free maintenance checks, or money-back guarantees. Fourth and last, make sure that you include all pertinent contact information. This may include the business' address and phone number, your hours of operation, and what, if any, credit cards you accept.

Make sure that you have proofread your ad multiple times and that you ask others to do so as well. This ad will appear exactly the way you write it for an entire year. If you are unsure about your ability to compile an effective advertisement, there are plenty of advertising agencies that are exclusively devoted to creating Yellow Page advertisements and placing them in the appropriate directories.

According to publishers, over sixty per cent of people consult the Yellow Pages regularly. It has become a conditioned response. Even with the advent of the internet, people are still more likely to pick up that handy book by the telephone instead of turning on their computers for specific business types. Thus, Yellow Pages advertisements work well for these businesses. They are proven to generate calls and produce sales.

Trade Shows

A trade show is a gathering of companies that are marketing similar products or companies that market different types of products but serve the same markets.

These shows allow companies to introduce their new products, meet customers, learn about trends in the industry, and attract new customers. At a typical national trade show, there will be 1000 companies exhibiting and 10,000 people attending the show. An exhibitor can realistically have 200 visitors to their booth per day.

Obviously, this is a great way to network with other businesses and increase your consumer base. You have the opportunity to create the all important first impression. You will not always have the opportunity to go into detail about your products and services, but you will get your proverbial foot in the door.

Trade shows are a great way for you to break away from the home office and interact with competition, consumers, and industry associates.

The key to finding the best shows for your organization is finding out which shows attract the biggest number of decision makers in your industry. To find out who attends a show, ask the show management for a demographic profile of their attendees. Check out the exhibitor list from last year.

You can also contact former exhibitors and ask for their impressions of the show. Make sure you ask show management how they plan to promote the show. Of course, you can always attend a prospective show yourself and form your own conclusions before committing to it for the next year.

Understanding Business Management

Now that you have you business plan in order and your finances in place, make sure that you have the skills necessary to lead your fledgling organization. In the past, a manager has been expected to maintain the status quo – in effect, to "keep a good thing going". However, in today's ever-changing market, managers have to be leaders. They have to be willing and able to continue learning and to come up with new ideas on a regular basis. Today's business executives must be forward-thinking teachers in order to keep their organizations competitive in today's marketplace.

Personality Traits of Leaders

One of the most important contributions made by the field of psychology to the business world has been the determination of the key traits of an effective leader. Raymond Cattell, an expert in the field of personality assessment, studied a group of military leaders in 1954 and came up with the following traits that they seemed to share:

- Emotional stability
- Dominance
- Enthusiasm
- Conscientiousness
- Social Boldness
- Tough-mindedness
- Self-assurance
- Compulsiveness

In addition to these traits, experts have found that today's leaders must also be able to motivate others and entice them to follow them in new directions. This ability seems to rely on a high energy level, intuitiveness, maturity, team orientation, empathy, and charisma.

Decision-Making Skills

As a leader of your company you will be called upon to make decisions on a regular basis. Here are some tips on making wise choices that will benefit you, your organization, and your bottom line.

1) Decide exactly what the decision is that needs to be made. Is there even a choice in the matter?
   Is this your decision to make?
2) Brainstorm for options and write them down.
3) Consider where you could find out more information about your dilemma. Possibilities include friends, family, clergy, co-workers, state and federal agencies, professional organizations, online services, newspapers, magazines, and books.
4) Look at the specifics of each option.
5) Sort through all of your alternatives and look at the values that come into play with the choice of each one. Keep the alternatives that allow you to use more of your values.
6) Consider which options are most realistic.
7) Evaluate the outcome and make any necessary adjustments.

Common Mistakes in Making Decisions

People who are making decisions have a tendency to rely too much on the advice of others and to discount their own opinions. Decisions can be made in which the decision-maker overestimates the value of information received from others or underestimates the information received from others. People also tend to hear only what they want to hear and see only what they want to see. Probably the most important thing that you should rely on is your emotional reaction and your gut feelings.

Customer Relations Skills

Customer service is of utmost importance to the success of any small business. In today's business world studies have shown that it can costs six times more to obtain a new customer than it does to keep an old one.

Seems that with customer service departments being outsourced, telephones being answered by computers, and email, customer service has become quite impersonal. This is where you can have an advantage over larger companies.

So how do you show your customers how important they are to you and insure their return? Treat people the way you would like to be treated. Single out the companies you have enjoyed doing business with and make a list of the specifics of the experience.

Another good approach is to act like you are the only contact the customer will ever have with the business (and in the case of a small, home-based business you may well be) and the company's image rests solely on your shoulders. Also pretend that each customer is your most important client. If the customer responds well to you and feels appreciated, then you have probably gained their loyalty.

Adjust your viewpoint. If you view customer service as an interruption to more important tasks that you must accomplish, the customer will sense that and will probably take their business to a place where they feel valued. Establish a rapport with your customers. Get to know people. Ask them about their health, their family, their job, etc. You cannot persuade someone to buy or do something if you cannot relate it to their life. You have to be able to show "what's in it for them".

When you are listening to a customer's complain, do not interrupt, and just let them vent their frustrations. If you stop them too soon, they will not be ready to consider your solutions. If possible offer alternative solutions to the problem, this will make the customer feel like they have some power over the situation. If you cannot resolve the problem, volunteer to get someone who can.

Be reliable, responsive, and credible. When you promise to do something, do it. When you are supposed to be somewhere at a specific time, be there. Go above and beyond what your customers expect by anticipating their needs. Above all, be truthful. Never lie or embellish when discussing your products or services with customers.

Five Elements That Support Good Customer Service

Communication –

   1 - Provide clear communication and confirm. Ask   people to repeat back to you what you have said. Avoid a condescending manner by stating, "I'm not sure I communicated that effectively, could you help me by telling me what I just said?' Reverse this suggestion when someone is talking to you. "Let me make sure I have this right," is a great way to repeat what you have heard for confirmation.

   Email is a mine field for miscommunication. While your message might seem perfectly logical to you, vocabulary and language, can easily be misconstrued. Conducting business with various cultures around the world can compound this issue. Before you hit the send button read your message a second time. When possible, have an independent third party read your letter and reiterate your meaning. This practice can help you develop better communication skills.

2- Provide professional and polite communication. While trends have led many in business to be sarcastic, comedic, or even caustic when emailing, stay on the high road. Remember email is a representation of you and your business.

Response – Respond to inquiries, questions, complaints, and messages as soon as possible.
Beginning in infancy, people have been conditioned to response. Agitation and aggravation can be dramatically reduced when people receive quick attention. If you don't already, learn to keep your calm even when others are agitated.
Inquiries and questions should be handled immediately. Set up an auto responder on your website to answer generic questions and collect contact information.

Expectations – Establish clear expectations by:

- Spelling out your project and services in detail.
- Asking questions, such as:

Is there anything else you are expecting in addition to what we have discussed?

How do you see this project working?

What are you

Action – Show customers that you take action.
Being a small business owner requires a decision maker who takes action. Keep a sense of urgency about everything you do. Studies have shown a sense of urgency was one common characteristic among most all self made millionaires. A sense of urgency will infiltrate your attitude when dealing with customers. They will appreciate your deliberateness.

Time - Manage time your time. Respect other's time by responding to them, meeting deadlines, and communicating when you cannot meet a deadline.

Entrepreneurship360 Online Entrepreneurship Courses

Our signature Entrepreneurship Program provides an excellent foundation for you to gain an understanding of the fundamental principals associated with operating a start-up business. Our live online courses and experienced instructors will help you to grow in your understanding of operating a new business venture, gain confidence, improve communication skills, and focus on the most pressing issues facing small businesses today.

The Program's curriculum consists of insightful courses which address key topics critical to the success of your new business. The courses are designed to have you actively participate in conducting research, designing and writing formal plans, i.e. feasibility plans, business plans, marketing plans, etc. Collaboration with the business community helps assure that this program is up-to-date, practical and challenging.

Our courses are second to none in formal business education, featuring:

- *Affordable courses*
- *Courses are open to anyone*
- *Small class sizes to encourage interactive discussions*
- *New classes starting monthly*
- *Informative lectures*

Visit us online at: www.entrepreneurship360online.com